The

Kissing

Flight Attendant

Charlotte Crumley Arrington

The Kissing Flight Attendant© 2021
Written By: Charlotte Crumley-Arrington

Library of Congress Cataloging – in- Publication Data has been applied for.

Paperback ISBN: 978-1-7373494-9-5

PRINTED IN THE UNITED STATES OF AMERICA.

Editing & Typesetting by Carla M. Dean, U Can Mark My Word
Front cover design by Christian Cuan

FIRST EDITION

TABLE OF CONTENTS

The

Kissing

Flight Attendant

Welcome to Flight 108

Welcome Aboard Flight 108! I am your Flight Attendant Instructor, and it is my pleasure to serve as your coach and angel of the air. Before we take off, allow me to introduce myself.

My name is Charlotte Crumley-Arrington aka The Kissing Flight Attendant. I served as a Flight Attendant with American Airlines and a Premiere Charter Airlines. I served as a Flight Attendant for fifteen years, and the passengers I encountered ranged from individuals who flew first-class to celebrity entertainers and athletes. It was always my dream to become a Flight Attendant because it afforded me the opportunity to travel and network while motivating others. Every flight was a different experience; however, each connected me to my purpose of service.

You see, as I shared in my book, *The Message 108: A Playbook to Manifesting & Achieving What Your Heart Desires*, becoming a Flight Attendant was the first profession I saw myself embarking on. Yet, after giving my candidacy speech for student president while attending Dana Jr. High School in Point Loma, California, I considered becoming a Motivational Speaker. I was intrigued with the idea of inspiring, motivating, and encouraging individuals to do what God put them here to do. It's something about the power of words—the ability to inform and inspire others to pursue their goals or purpose. The good thing about being a Flight Attendant is that I could use my gift of communication and motivating while serving passengers. You would be surprised how many airline passengers hope to have a friendly Flight Attendant— especially if they are flying solo and have no one to converse with during their travel. The Flight Attendant typically steps in to listen, laugh, and learn what passengers need to make their flight enjoyable. So, when you think about it, becoming my junior high school's president and honing my speaking skills prepared me for a career as a Flight Attendant. Being able to communicate with a smile—and from the heart—will make your journey an experience you will never forget.

Before sharing all of the wonderful things there is to

know about becoming a Flight Attendant, I must warn you that this job is not for those individuals who are afraid of heights, hate to travel, and expect to earn a high salary. If you are that person, close the book and pass it on to one of your friends or a family member! Being a Flight Attendant comes with some sacrifices. For many, it's a job beyond their wildest dreams, and for others, it turns out to be the worst job of their life. There's a saying about careers in aviation: "It's either in your blood, or it's not." Fortunately, it does not take long to figure out which applies to you.

You may be thinking, *If this book is for those who want to pursue a career as a Flight Attendant, why is she trying to discourage me?* Great question! As a coach, I am committed to giving you both sides of the equation so that you are fully equipped with the information needed to make a sound decision. I loved being a Flight Attendant. Many people see this profession as glamorous because of the travel benefits and opportunities to meet new people. However, I would be remiss if I did not educate you on the flip side of those perks. When it comes to being a Flight Attendant, here are a few things you can expect:

- According to the U.S. Bureau of Labor Statistics' Occupational Outlook Handbook, the 2020 median pay for flight attendants was $59,000.

- New Flight Attendants are always on call (reserved) because they don't know which flight will require their services.
- Flight Attendants usually fly 75 to 100 hours a month and spend another 50 hours on the ground preparing flights, writing reports, and waiting for aircraft to arrive.
- Taking unexpected time off from work is extremely difficult because they need to find someone to cover their flight.
- Jet lag can be a real problem when working as a Flight Attendant, especially when traveling over multiple time zones.

As you see, being a Flight Attendant can be taxing on both your physical and mental health. So, even though the uniform looks pretty, the job requires you to be all smiles––even when your feet are hurting and you're ready to go home.

So, are you still interested in becoming a flight attendant? Yes? Great! Then let's proceed...

In this book, *The Kissing Flight Attendant*, I will share everything you need to know about becoming a Flight Attendant. Even though the laws and regulations are updated frequently, this book will serve as your introduction while providing essential information on qualifications, training, and reporting to work. I will also share the history of this profession, along with some personal stories of what life is like traveling the friendly skies.

I have been very successful on and off the aircraft throughout my career, and I want the same testimony for you. It is my sheer hope that if being a Flight Attendant is your ultimate goal, you use this book as your resource. I have not only shared my personal knowledge, but I have researched and provided as much current information to ensure the information is up to date.

Before we taxi from the jet way, I have one more question to ask you: Are you ready to travel on Flight 108? Yes? Great! Then, ladies and gentlemen, the Kissing Flight Attendant has turned on the "Fasten Your Seatbelt" sign. It's time to buckle up. Flight 108 is ready for takeoff. Next stop, your dream job as a First-Class Flight Attendant.

Flight Attendants,

please prepare the cabin for takeoff . . .

Everyone Called Is Not Qualified

Welcome to the first stop of your flight attendant journey! I hope you are as excited as I am and looking forward to learning the ins and outs of being a Flight Attendant. At this stop, we will look at the history of this profession and the standard qualifications every candidate must possess. As with any job, Flight Attendants have rules and regulations—theirs governed by the Federal Aviation Administration (FAA). For those who may not know what or who the FAA is, they issue and enforce regulations and minimum standards covering manufacturing, operating, and maintaining aircraft. They also certify airmen and airports that serve air carriers. Even though you are employed by the airline as a Flight Attendant, your education and certification are gained through the FAA.

As a scholar, understanding the history and importance of this profession is key. For me, it allowed me to understand that this career requires great people skills and analytical skills. There is a quote by British statesman Winston Churchill that I live by when achieving new adventures: *Those that fail to learn from history are doomed to repeat it.* I learned about his quote for a speech I gave representing my freshman speech class at Howard University. This quote also propelled me to Minor in US History. I know many of you have heard this before and find purpose in it when it comes to learning who you are and tracing your generational lineage to process where you're going. However, let's consider that same reasoning but with understanding the purpose of the job and what tools and attributes you need to master to become successful as a Flight Attendant. For me, learning any job's background is rewarding. Plus, it gives you more confidence during your interview while sharing why you are the best candidate for the job.

TYPES OF FLIGHT ATTENDANT JOBS

Before we jump into the material, let's briefly look at the two types of flight attendant jobs.

Commercial Airlines

Generally, commercial airlines carry passengers or cargo for hire or compensation. These flights depart and arrive from federal airports. This type of airline makes the bulk of their money transporting cargo. For example, my good friend worked for an airline as a ramp agent, and he would share stories of having to load whales for national aquariums, large amounts of money for big banks, etc. During your first week of training, your trainer will inform you of the aircraft's cargo and how it is factored into the flight plan.

Charter Airlines

Charter airlines are pay-for-hire airlines that provide private passenger travel services. These flights depart and arrive at private airports called Flight Base Offices (FBOs). These airports are located off to the side of the main airport and have their own boarding area, lounge, and private TSA for hire that the paying client staffs. They use the same runway as the commercial airlines depending on the size of the aircraft.

Throughout my career, I have been blessed to work on both types of carriers. Even though both have passengers you have to serve, you engage more with the passengers on a charter flight, which is more of a private flight. Thus, working this type of flight gives you the opportunity to network, converse, and enjoy the moment. Charter flights are great, especially when the passengers are amazing.

THE HISTORY OF FLIGHT ATTENDANTS

The history of the Flight Attendant is astonishing. It was derived from similar positions on passenger ships and planes, where stewards served the passengers as they traveled. With the same concept, once airplanes were created and airlines emerged, stewards were needed to help maintain order and provide safety. Many people think being a Flight Attendant is a predominately female job, but truth be told, it did not start out that way. The first Flight Attendant was a male by the name of Heinrich Kubis. He served on the LZ 10 Schwaben aircraft that serviced Berlin to Friedrichshafen in 1912. It wasn't until 1930 that a woman Flight Attendant was allowed in the air. Ellen Church, who was a trained nurse and pilot, convinced Boeing Air Transport that using nurses as Flight Stewardesses would increase safety and help convince passengers that flying was safe. She embarked on a Boeing 80A for a 20-hour flight from Oakland/San Francisco to Chicago with 13 stops and 14 passengers, and thus, women Flight Attendants were birthed. Since those first flights, both women and men have traveled throughout history to take what started as mimicking passenger trains and boat crews to evolving the experience of air travel. Flight Attendants have a rich history of growth from the duties and even their job title. Did you know Flight Attendants were not always referred to by such name? In the beginning, they were called Couriers and were the sons of businessmen who financed the airlines. After the stock market crash in 1929, they were replaced by the copilot. The copilot was required to assist the pilot in command to fly the plane and then serve food and drinks when it was safe to leave the captain alone. As air travel improved, the needs of passengers were assessed, and airlines started hiring Stewards. They were responsible for all the passengers' needs, including helping passengers board, assisting with baggage, serving refreshments, and assuring all cigars and cigarettes were put out.

As women became Stewardesses and joined the ranks of male stewards, the treatment of women was more restrictive and unrealistic. For example, "airlines as part of their hiring practices required women to take an oath that prohibited them from marriage and children." (avstop.com) Defying this oath would lead to immediate termination. To further challenge airlines' restrictions, African Americans and men began seeking employment in the field, which threw another curveball. Met with many protests. Mohawk Airlines became the first airline to hire an African American woman in December of 1957. The very next year, Ruth Carol Taylor made history on the flight from Ithaca to New York. However, due to a "marriage" violation, Mrs. Taylor was terminated. Thankfully, the many laws and regulations that shaped the profession have since been deemed unconstitutional or relaxed, such as:

- In 1968, the Equal Employment Opportunity Commission (EEOC) declared age restrictions on flight attendants' employment to be illegal sex discrimination under Title VII of the Civil Rights Act of 1964.
- Also, in 1968, the EEOC ruled that sex was not a bona fide occupational requirement to be a flight attendant.
- The restriction of only hiring women was lifted at all airlines in 1971 due to the decisive court case of Diaz vs. Pan Am.
- The no-marriage rule was eliminated throughout the US airline industry by the 1980s.
- The last such broad categorical discrimination—the weight restrictions—were relaxed in the 1990s through litigation and negotiations.

As you can see, passenger safety on an aircraft came with a price. The only requirement that remains from the past is the weight and height. Prior to today, a candidate's weight and height were measured during the interview. Humiliating, right? Can you imagine being interviewed by a panel of managers and then asked to step on a scale to be weighed? Until this was outlawed, it was required of a potential Flight Attendant. Today, they measure the candidate's weight by their ability to fasten their seatbelt while sitting on the jump seat. This test is typically conducted during the first few days of training and one you must pass. In addition, the measuring of height is determined by the candidate's ability to place a bag in the overhead bin without using the edge of the seat to assist in lifting them up. Aren't you grateful to be considering this career in the 2020s instead of back when the requirements for Flight Attendants were more stringent? This is a great time and presents a lot of opportunities for you to become a Flight Attendant.

Now that you have a better understanding of the history of Flight Attendants, let's dive into the qualifications.

QUALIFICATIONS

The qualifications to become a Flight Attendant are

pretty simple today. According to the U.S. Bureau of Labor Statistics' Occupational Outlook Handbook, Flight Attendants (2021), the qualifications of becoming a flight attendant are as follows:

- A high school diploma or the equivalent and work experience in customer service.
- Must be at least 18 years old and be eligible to work in the United States.
- One or two years of work experience in a service occupation prior to applying.
- Have a valid passport.
- Pass a background check and drug test.
- Vision that is correctable to at least 20/40.
- Conform to height requirements set by the airline.
- Pass a medical evaluation.
- Present a professional appearance and does not have visible tattoos, body piercings, or an unusual hairstyle or makeup.

As we all know, these qualifications are based on the standards set by the government. However, every airline has its own set of qualifications that keep their company's reputation excellent. Airlines are one of the largest monopolies competing for your business; thus, many will set their standards above or below the legal standard to make it easy to hire employees. Following are the Flight Attendant requirements for the top three airlines, according to The Travel Academy.

United Airlines

United flight attendants must be at least 21 years old at the time of application and have a valid passport. Height-wise, attendants should be between 5'2" and 6'3" without shoes. They do not allow facial piercings or visible tattoos––even if concealed. A high school diploma is required, with two or more years of college preferred. A flight attendant working for United Airlines should be able to read, write, speak and understand English. Speaking a second language fluently is not required but is considered an asset. The airline has bases in Chicago, Denver, Houston, Los Angeles, Newark, San Francisco, Washington Dulles, Boston, Cleveland, Las Vegas, and Honolulu.

Delta Airlines

Delta flight attendants must be at least 21 years old and have a high school diploma or GED. Attendants must be willing to work a flexible schedule and be fluent in English (speaking, reading, and writing). Facial piercings, multiple earlobe piercings, and earlobe plugs aren't permitted.

21

Likewise, they don't allow any unnatural hair colors or nail decals. For men, facial hair is permitted but must be neatly trimmed and fall within their length requirements. New hires are expected to complete an 8-week training in Atlanta, Georgia. The airline has bases in Atlanta, Boston, Detroit, Los Angeles, Minneapolis, New York, Salt Lake City, and Seattle.

Southwest Airlines

Southwest will consider an application if the person is at least 20 years old when they apply. Visible body and facial piercings are not allowed, and only two pairs of earrings are allowed in the earlobe—with limitations on size and length. Southwest's tattoo policy is a little more flexible than other airlines in that tattoos are allowed as long as they are covered when in uniform. A high school diploma is required, and college coursework or a degree is an asset. A flight attendant working for Southwest Airlines should be able to read, write, speak, and understand English. Speaking a second language fluently is not required for every flight. The airline has bases in Atlanta, Baltimore, Chicago, Dallas, Denver, Houston, Las Vegas, Orlando, Oakland, and Phoenix.

APPLYING FOR THE JOB

Based on the above list, are you qualified? If you answered yes, it's time for you to apply. But first, allow me to offer you another word of advice. When applying for the Flight Attendant job, it would be beneficial to know who you are, what you want, and your best attributes. Knowing the answer to these things will lessen your chances of being eliminated from the competition. If your resume does not speak to their customer service mission, you'll likely be eliminated. And just a heads up—make sure to highlight your listening skills, flexibility, willingness to relocate, and customer service experience in your cover letter.

Listening Skills — Good listening skills are essential. You must be able to follow directions and serve. Failure to note this key quality may result in the discarding of your application. So, make sure you highlight this essential skill and provide examples.

Flexibility — Are you able to adapt quickly? Being a Flight Attendant requires you to be prepared for delays, re-routing, and incidents while in flight. Are you flexible enough to change course, or do you need things to run on schedule? Flexibility and being able to adjust to a change at the last minute are essential to the job.

Relocation — Being able to relocate is a major commitment to this profession. You will be asked questions about relocating fifty different ways during the interview; the moment you hesitate to respond is when you will no longer be considered for the position. The first time you will be required to relocate is when you have to complete training at the company's headquarters, which is more than likely not located in your hometown.

Customer Service — If you don't already know, a Flight Attendant's primary responsibilities are passenger safety and providing good customer service. The saying is, *"The customer is always right."* Don't you just love that? Your prior customer service experience plays a big part in the airline's decision to hire you. How you communicate with human resources before, during, and after the interview is important. After completing your application, you will be invited to an in-person interview to introduce you to the hiring team. The interviewers will watch you from the time you walk in—assessing how you interact, sit down, respond in conversation, your facial expressions, and most importantly, your appearance and body language. All of these things are associated with customer service. So, during the interviewing process, make sure you give eye contact, listen intently, and be mindful of how you answer the questions asked.

As I've mentioned before, applying for the position is nothing more than a process of elimination. The airline will offer only the best of the best the opportunity to attend the official interviews. But, if you thought you would be done after this, you are mistaken. Sorry, love! It's more to this process; there are at least three interviews that you must get through before being hired. So, dry clean your outfit and get ready because it's time for you to land the job by verifying who you are and gaining their trust.

Time to Land the Job

Way to go! You completed the application process, and it has been decided you are one of the best candidates for the job. You have been notified, and now it's time to start the three-level interview process. Yes, I said three interviews. If you haven't learned already, everything about becoming a Flight Attendant is a process. There is no such thing as one and done with obtaining this position. With all the responsibilities of Flight Attendants, it's always many options, and they do them all—even the ones we might have missed. Think about it, passengers' safety is in your hands from the moment the first passenger steps onto the aircraft until the last one disembarks. So, pack your patience as we discuss the interview process.

When it comes to the interview, be prepared to answer questions about your employment history, educational background, skills and qualifications for the job, and your goals for the future. In addition, you may be asked questions pertaining to personality—behavioral and situational—to understand not only your values and morals as a person but how involved or detailed oriented you are when it comes to handling situations, both expected and unexpected. The following sample questions will help you as you prepare for the interview.

- If two passengers were having a dispute over one seat, what would be your method for resolving the issue?
- Do you feel comfortable in new environments and situations?
- How have you resolved a challenging situation with a co-worker in the past?
- What are your customer service strengths?
- What was your favorite flight experience?
- What are the first things you would do in an emergency while in flight?
- What would you do if someone afraid of flying started panicking?
- How would you handle a passenger who refuses to

comply with Flight Attendant instructions during takeoff and/or landing?

THE INTERVIEW STEPS

Now that you are prepared for the interview, let's dive into the process. As stated above, there are three steps to the interview: group interview, one-on-one interview, and a final interview at the corporate headquarters. First impressions are everything, so let's start with what is highly recommended for you to wear if you want to remain a viable candidate for the Flight Attendant position.

Dress Code – For the in-person interview, women should dress in a black or navy blue pants or skirt suit with a white blouse, stockings, black or navy blue closed-toe flats or heels, no buckles or designs. If your hair falls below your shoulder, make sure it's pulled up into a neat bun. Makeup should be worn with a preference for red lipstick. This was the original color mandated by airlines because it was thought to make your mouth more visible and draw people's attention to you while you're giving the safety demonstration.

For men, the dress code is a black or navy blue suit, a black or navy blue belt, a white shirt with a long necktie, black or navy blue dress socks, black or navy blue shoes, no buckles or designs. If you have long hair, put it in a sexy man bun or, better yet, get a haircut. You can grow it back once off probation and then wear it in a sexy man bun.

- **Group Interview** ~ Once it has been determined you meet the job requirements, you will be invited to a group interview. This is when you will be interviewed by a panel that usually consists of three people. Their primary focus is to rate you on how well you perform under pressure and your ability to work as a team player. They will also observe your ability to answer questions as well as how good you are at listening and following directions. Do you answer the questions with confidence? Are you focused and a good listener? These things will be determined during the group interview.
- **One-on-one Interview** ~ Once you pass the group interview, a one-on-one interview will be conducted to review further your credentials, personality, and ability to perform the job. If the local level management and human resources like you, you are then invited to the corporate office for the final step during the interviewing process. If you make it to the corporate office, you are one inch from the goal line. At this point, the ball is in your

court. Don't fumble it.

- **Corporate Interview** ~ When you receive the phone call inviting you to attend an interview at the corporate office, the airline has confirmed their interest in you. However, before making their final decision, they want to see how you blend in. Do you fit the corporate's motto? Does your personality exhibit the company's values and reputation? Does your demeanor make you stand out? Does your vibe offer a warm feeling for customers?

The airline will arrange your travel, but keep this in mind. From the moment you arrive at the airport until you depart at the end of the interview process, everyone will be watching you.

The ticket agent is aware of who you are, and they are watching to see how you interact with people. The Flight Attendants on the aircraft are watching to see how you behave during the flight. Quiet as it's kept, they are monitoring you in order to give the corporate office a report confirming whether or not you are a good candidate. And please, whatever you do on that flight, do not order an alcoholic beverage.

Once you arrive at the airport, a van will transport you to the corporate office. Again, prepare to have all eyes on you. I mean, everyone will be watching, observing, and examining your every move. You will be shown to a room with the other candidates, and they will begin the interview process. After the interview process, if they feel you will be a great asset, they will give you a medical packet to complete your eye exam, hearing test, and drug test. Once completed, you will be given your flight details to return home, and that is when the real waiting game begins.

If all comes back positive and they decide to hire you, you will receive a provisional offer of employment. It is a provisional offer because you have to successfully complete training to be officially hired. Let me forewarn you that, more than likely, training will be unpaid. However, the airlines will cover the expenses for your lodging and meals during training.

By now, you are probably thinking, "Charlotte, this is too much." Trust me, I know. However, if being a Flight Attendant is something you really want, you will see this process through and celebrate once you get your "wings."

For the sake of this book, let's claim you have already received a provisional offer. Well, that means it's time to attend training at the airline's corporate office. Let's go!

THE TRAINING PERIOD

The training period differs between all airlines. However, be prepared to be away from home for at least three to six weeks.

- For the major airlines like American, United, and Delta, training will be at least six weeks because you have to learn every aircraft on the fleet and test out on them at 90% or better.
- If you chose an airline like Southwest that uses two aircraft styles or a charter airline, training will be three to four weeks since they do not have a variety of planes.

When it comes to packing, don't overstuff your suitcase with too many clothes, planning to change your outfit every day. You will be sized for your uniform during the second week of training, and that will be your work attire for the remaining weeks of training. This will be a moment of realization, so get ready! Along with my fellow classmates, I felt like Cinderella with all of the measuring, hemming, and styling that came with obtaining our first Flight Attendant uniform. The first time you put on that uniform, you will feel extremely excited, humbled, and like you're floating on cloud nine. It will be a moment of reckoning that your dream is finally coming true.

During training, you must be as focused as a racehorse, meaning put on your blinders and keep your eyes on the prize. Ask questions if you are unsure about a lesson. Take notes. Start a study group.

During my first week of training at American Airlines, we went over the history of aviation and the company and learned about our first aircraft. That Friday, we had a test, and as soon as that evening, people were leaving. My roommate was one of those people. Every lesson or lecture is accompanied by a test that you must pass with a score of 90% or better. Anything below that, you will have to pack your backs to return home. They give you one opportunity to retake the test, but if your score is still below 90%, you must exit stage left.

Why are the testing standards so rigid? I'm happy you asked. Think about it this way, being a Flight Attendant makes you responsible for the lives on the aircraft, which includes your crew members. Every passenger's life on that aircraft is in your hands. For example, if a passenger has a heart attack, you must know how to immediately work the Automated External Defibrillator (AED). Every second counts. You don't have time to read the directions or call someone for help. There may come a time when you are faced with a life-or-death situation, and you may be the only Flight Attendant in the vicinity of the emergency. You must always be ready to go into action and possibly save a life.

Throughout the training, you will learn a new aircraft and the other responsibilities of being a Flight Attendant. You will cover areas on:

- Preflight procedures
- Inflight/Post flight procedures
- Emergency procedures
- Flight Attendant training
- Checklists, forms, and appendices
- Food preparation
- Sequence of service

Another thing they drive home in training is that your focus while on the aircraft should not only be on the passengers. As a Flight Artendant, you are also responsible for the cabin and cockpit crews. You are the pulse of the entire operation while in flight. Thus, another reason why learning and passing your exams are essential.

One other thing, make sure you pack your bathing suit because you will have to practice water drills in order to master how to open the life raft and pull passengers out of the water into the raft if there is ever an emergency landing over water. This is where teamwork and leadership skills come into play because should you find yourself in this situation, you have to take command and lead everyone to safety.

Upon completion of training, there is a graduation ceremony, which you can invite your family to attend to join in your celebration. You will be given your wings during graduation, which signifies you are officially a Flight Attendant and part of your airline's family. I remember receiving my first set of wings from American Airlines and becoming a part of the Kiwi Club. The Kiwi Club is a unique philanthropic social group that ties former and current American Airlines stewardesses and Flight Attendants to a network of friendship, community service, and mutual support. I will also say that when I received my second set of wings, I felt the same excitement and wore them with just as much pride and excitement because I loved being a Flight Attendant. I was on a level I did not know existed; my wings once again were earned and not given.

FLIGHT ATTENDANT CERTIFICATE OF DEMONSTRATED PROFICIENCY

All Flight Attendants must be certified by the Federal Aviation Administration. Flight Attendants are certified for specific aircraft types and must take new training for each type of aircraft on which they will work. The Federal Aviation Administration website states:

"In the fall of 2003, Congress established a flight attendant certification requirement in the Vision 100-Century of Aviation Reauthorization Act. The Act requires that after December 11, 2004, no person may serve as a flight attendant aboard an aircraft of an air carrier unless that person holds a Certificate of Demonstrated Proficiency (certificate) issued by the FAA. Flight attendants are not required to carry the certificate. If requested, flight attendants shall present their certificate to the FAA, the National Transportation Safety Board, or another Federal agency within a reasonable period of time after the date of request. The FAA policy for "a reasonable period of time" is 15 days."

So, you see, all the rigorous training you went through was mandated by something bigger than the airline itself. In addition to receiving your wings upon graduation, you will receive an FAA card acknowledging you have completed training. I'm so proud of you!

Congratulations! You Are Now a Flight Attendant

You've made it through and have officially earned the title of Flight Attendant! How do you feel? Is wearing that uniform everything you dreamt it would be? After all of these years, I can still remember when I finished training. I was super excited and ready to hit the skies. My first position as a Flight Attendant was working in first-class, which simply means I worked in the #1 position, aka first-class. Also, the first-class Flight Attendant is the "leader" and communicates with the ground crew, provides the flight briefing to the crew, reads the safety demo announcement, and coordinates with the catering staff.

I freaked out when I saw my schedule right out of training and found out I was assigned as a first-class Flight Attendant. Being new in the game, it's the luck of the draw; once you receive your schedule, you get what you get. However, as I embarked on my position, I realized I knew more than I thought. Training had prepared us to serve in any position on any aircraft. So, my nervousness eased, and I stepped into my answered prayer because failure is never an option.

I worked turns from Chicago to New York and met many celebrities and business people. Meeting people was most exciting for me, especially when they were people who I listened to on the radio, watched in movies, and had seen on television. The only time I found myself star struck was when I met NHL coach Wayne Gretzky and NBA player Ray Allen. There were some exciting moments when I reviewed the flight manifest and saw who would be on my flight.

One night on reserves, I got a call to ferry the plane to Los Angeles to pick up a client and take them to Toronto. Once the whole crew arrived, we asked the Lead Flight Attendant who we were flying, and she said, "Some Hip-Hop artist named Drake." I had to call my kids to find out who he was, and baby—they were so excited! My son wanted to know if Nicki Minaj was traveling with him. At that point, I became excited to meet him because my children were excited. He was an hour late for his flight, which was typical when servicing people in the entertainment industry. That was a blessing because we got called off reserves at 10:00 p.m., it gave us a chance to get some rest once we set the appetizers out and prepared their spaces. So, we didn't mind their lateness one bit. Once it was time to board the aircraft, I would greet them as though they were my friends. Some may have thought I was excessively friendly; others may have questioned if I was crazy. Regardless of what they thought of me, I had a ball. I was living my dream. They were a guest on my aircraft, and I was honored that God chose me to be in the presence of people who I looked up to and respected for following their dreams, as well.

I remember when I would see celebrities passing by in the airport. I would speak to them as if they were my friends, and they would have a look in their eyes as if to say, "I don't know this woman." They would either speak back or keep walking. I found this very amusing because we see these people in movies and on television and can sometimes become so connected with them that we start to think we know them personally. In my mind, I would think they were my friends, but then I would laugh once I realized they were not. They are celebrities.

Fair warning, when you see your first person of influence, you will get stuck and have to mentally slap yourself back into reality. Just remember they are not your friends. You know them via their jobs, and that's it. Still, embrace the moment. It's one of the amusing perks of the job. Okay, back to the topic!

During your final weeks of training, you will get to request your choice of three bases that you will report to one week after training. Based on your preferences, they will choose one and let you know once you have completed and passed your final exam. You will be able to request a base change after you have completed probation.

Once you complete your training, you may have to relocate depending on the bases available. However, if there is a base available close to your home, you will have the option to commute. But guess what? You are a Flight Attendant now! So, celebrate your amazing achievement.

After you are assigned to your base, you will be placed on a 90-day probation—no different than another job. They will monitor your job performance and make sure you adhere to the dress code during this time. But on the 91st day, you can let your hair down, grow your sexy man bun if you're a male, and relax a little. Be yourself and enjoy the journey.

Now, if you have decided you want to commute to your base, let me warn you that commuting is very stressful. Personally, I would not recommend it. You should not have to jump over hurdles just to get to work. Plus, the airline industry is 24 hours a day, 7 days a week, and being a flight attendant is not your typical 9–5 job. Some shifts are as long as 16 hours! You may be scheduled early mornings, late nights, and holidays. On top of that, you'll have a minimum of 11 days off each month. Who would want to commute with that kind of life? That would be me. I commuted most of my career, and at times, I dreaded it. It became costly, stressful, and it mentally and physically wore me out. Think of commuting like this:

You live in another city, so you have to get to the airport and fly standby. Flying standby means you can only get on the plane if there are empty seats remaining after all paying customers have boarded. If you have flown this way, you know it is not a guarantee and can result in you spending a whole day in the airport. Is this how you want to impress your boss? You can't get a flight to your base, you miss your show time, and now you have to get a hotel until you can fly out.

Another thing to consider when deciding if you are going to relocate is your work schedule. New Flight Attendants spend the majority of their time on reserve. Reserve means you are on call. The airlines typically staff all flights in advance, so getting an aircraft to serve will become the "hurry up and wait" process. Flight Attendants usually remain on reserve for at least one year, and in some cities, it may take five years or longer to advance from reserve to permanent status. I can remember getting notified at the last minute to report to work when the airlines needed more crew because someone called out sick or needed me to complete an in-process flight that got stuck due to maintenance or weather. Can you imagine living in Nevada, and your base is in Los Angeles, and getting a call at four o'clock in the morning telling you to report to work at eight a.m.? You cannot tell your supervisor that you will be late; lateness is not an option, nor calling in sick. Word of advice, do not call in sick. It's better to be sent home ill than call in sick.

CREW ON DUTY

Even though this book is about becoming a Flight Attendant, they are only as successful as the entire crew aboard an aircraft. When people say, "There is no I in team," they are speaking about the roles of Flight Attendants. They have to work, communicate, and trust everyone on that team. They have to listen, provide, serve, and protect while in the air or even when grounded. The Flight Attendant is your direct point of contact while on an aircraft, but do you know the other team members? No? Well, let's review them quickly.

- **Cabin Crew** — the cabin crew is everyone who works onboard an aircraft. This includes the flight attendants, senior flight attendants, pursers, pilots, copilot, and flight engineer.

- **Flight Crew** — the flight crew are those involved with flying a plane. This includes the pilots, the flight engineer, and the navigator. You can find them in the cockpit.

Even though everyone has separate responsibilities, no flight would operate smoothly if all crew members were not aboard. Thus, teamwork is essential, as well as getting to know your team. You should know each other's strengths, weaknesses, skills, and abilities. You never know who you might need to call in case of an emergency.

THE BENEFITS

Benefits! This topic alone is one of the main reasons why people seek a career in air travel. Do you and your family fly for free with your present job? Do you get paid time off? Flight Attendants get to travel on an all-expense-paid vacation in the name of work every day. You would be surprised how many questions I get when it comes to being a Flight Attendant. How do you distinguish between the truth and myths? As someone who lived this life for fifteen years, I am here to share the facts with you so you will know exactly what you are getting yourself into when you decide to become a Flight Attendant. I always refer to this as a job with vacation privileges. Once you get to your destination, you are off duty and able to enjoy yourself.

Once you've passed the probationary period, you will be allotted travel passes for your family and friends. Now let's be clear here, these travel passes are not free. You, as the employee, will pay for all flight taxes out of your paycheck for your travel and the travel passes you designate to your family and friends. I have seen Flight Attendants receive a paycheck for $0.00 because their family or friends utilized the travel passes, and the deductions took their whole paycheck. I received a few of those checks myself, and that's when I realized I had to be selective about who I provided my passes to and get the money for the taxes before turning over any tickets. I mean, who wants to live with no money so others can fly free? This benefit is a great reward, but if not used correctly, it can cost you.

The other unique thing with travel passes is that the passengers are flying on standby. Again, standby means you have to wait until the gate agent confirms that all paying passengers have claimed their seat and there is an extra seat for you to fly. There have been instances where standby passengers were permitted to board the plane because seats were available during the boarding process, but then, the tardy passenger who paid for their flight arrived at the gate. Do you know what happens in that situation? You got it! The standby passenger has to get up so the paying passenger can have their seat.

The whole standby process is an anxious and humbling experience. Imagine waiting until after all passenger's board the aircraft, only to hear that there are no more seats left. Not only that, but it is your third flight rejection that day. It happens, especially during the holidays and winter season. I always made sure to tell my people to have a plan B in case they did not get out of the city while flying standby.

While we may want to show our love and appreciation

to our family and friends by sharing our flight privileges with them, it's not always a good idea. Their misbehavior and bad attitude may cause you to lose your flight privileges for a whole year. So, be careful who you allow to use your flight privileges because that's what they are— —a privilege.

In addition to travel passes, there are other benefits Flight Attendants receive:

- **Free Flights and Travel Opportunities** — We've discussed this previously, but for many, this is the biggest and best benefit of them all. In addition to traveling while working, some airlines allow Flight Attendants to earn additional mileage while being repositioned to where the aircraft is departing. This happens a lot with being a charter Flight Attendant. For example, I was the lead F/A (flight attendant) for the Chicago Bulls and lived in Phoenix, Arizona. The company would book my flights to Chicago on a commercial airline, and I accumulated the mileage points and used them for my personal travel or gift them to my children. As a Flight Attendant, you can also fly jump seat, which means you can sit on the jump seat if one is available and all of the passenger seats are full.

- **Flexible Schedule** — Flight Attendants have unique and flexible scheduling. Many work three days per week, and those with seniority can pick their schedules first and discard their trips first. Aviation is a 100% seniority business, and the senior F/As rule the nest when it comes to the highest pay, best schedule, and most flexibility. Depending on the airline is depending on one's seniority. For example, a F/A who has been flying for 20 years may be considered a junior at a major base. As a junior F/A, you will get a lot of stop-and-go trips, not-so-fun layovers, and not-so-great pay. It's all about paying your dues and putting in the time, and in due season, you will reach the status of senior F/A—with the best trips, best layovers, and best pay.

- **Food Expense Reimbursement** — Another source of income for a F/A is per-diem. Once you sign in for your trip, you start earning a per-diem per hour that is slated for your meals while on the road. Some airlines will give you two separate checks—one for flight hours and one for per-diem. Your flight hours start accumulating once the wheels depart from the gate. In addition to per-diem, the F/A will receive crew meals depending on the length of the flight, which is provided by catering along with the meals for the passengers. And in case you're wondering, yes, you can munch on the in-flight snacks and even take a few to your room for later.

- **Overnight Hotel Stays** — Most flights require the crew to stay overnight in another city or country before the trip is considered complete and returns to the base. When traveling overnight for work, hotel stays are free for crew members and another opportunity to accumulate reward points for future stays at the hotel chain while on a personal trip. Although the pay is not that great as a F/A, the amazing benefits allow you to live as though you earn twice as much. Hotel stays are a lot of fun because there's usually a restaurant, bar, and sometimes a jumping nightclub on the premises or in the vicinity. More than likely, another person from the crew will want to hang out. This is what I liked to call a vacation in the name of work. Then there are those hotels that have nice pools and lounging areas. I thoroughly enjoyed those perks. Sometimes mothers feel guilty for having fun, but that wasn't my case when I lounged by the hotel pool. What made it even sweeter was that I was getting paid for it. One thing, though. Be careful. Once the crew (especially the commercial crew) arrives at the hotel, everyone usually goes their separate ways, but it's important to communicate with at least one crew member, especially if you plan on leaving the hotel.

- **Ability to Manage Own Self** — Flight Attendants travel without a manager on board; thus, they manage their own responsibilities. They need to follow airline training and guidelines and work with a crew team, but Flight Attendants can self-direct their daily tasks. That's a major plus and one that I loved so much! Imagine having a job where once you get off the plane, your work is done. No reports need to be filled out unless there was an incident, and no having to wait to be relieved from your duties. You never take your work home with you, and each day of work, you have another chance to make a great first impression with those who fly on your airline.

- **Health insurance** — Most airlines offer great health packages to employees. These can include medical, vision, dental, and life insurance policies for flight attendants and their dependents. These plans may also include health savings accounts and other medical benefits.

- **Retirement plans** — Many Flight Attendants receive retirement benefits or saving plans. This benefit helps employees plan and budget for the future.

- **Compensation** — Flight Attendants receive a competitive salary for their work. The average Flight Attendant makes $36,866 per year, working the minimum hours per month. I have known a few F/A who earned over $100k, but this number varies depending on the airline, experience, and amount of time worked.

COMMERCIAL VS CHARTER

We touched on this in a previous chapter, but now that you are a Flight Attendant, let's discuss the two. When it comes to being a Flight Attendant, you don't only have to work a commercial airline. You can opt to work with charter plane companies, too. I had the honor to work both during my career.

Commercial Aviation

The one thing I can say about commercial flights is that they are very organized. You typically have a schedule where you work a variation of fifteen days on and fifteen days off. Commercial aviation is the part of civil aviation (both general aviation and scheduled airline services) that involves operating aircraft to transport passengers or multiple cargo loads. This is where your Delta, United, American, and other airlines fit. They get their rules and regulations from the Federal Aviation Administration (FAA). The Federal Aviation Administration (FAA) is the United States Department of Transportation agency responsible for the regulation and oversight of civil aviation within the U.S. and the operation and development of the National Airspace System. The FAA website https://www.faa.gov/ is a great way to learn more about the rules and regulations of the crew members and the passengers.

Charter

When it comes to charter flights, things are a bit different. According to Stratos Jet Charter, Inc., a charter flight is defined as "an unscheduled flight that is not part of a regular airline routing. With a charter flight, you rent the entire aircraft and can determine departure/arrival, menu, locations, and service flow." Moreover, charter flights are most popular because they are private flights. Meaning, the person who is booking the charter flight gets to say who boards the aircraft. Charter airlines usually depart from a Flight Base Office (FBO) located on the other side of the airport field. The best part of being a passenger on these flights is having privacy and luxury all on one plane. It gets no better than this. However, the FAA monitors these companies closer than commercial airlines, but the rules are more moderate than commercial.

In my experience, both of them have their advantages and disadvantages, but they are both enjoyable. When a Flight Attendant on commercial flights, I was typically home after three or four days on the road, and I received flight benefits not only for myself but for my friends and family, as well. However, your road time is much longer with charter flights, and there are no flight privileges unless the company makes a deal for you with a commercial airline. But you do remember me saying the FAA rules for charter flights are more moderate. Thus, passengers are more relaxed once the plane is in the air, and the environment feels like you're hosting a party with friends even though you are working. The service on charter flights is fast-paced, nonstop, lavish, and tiring.

The pay is quite different for both. Commercial airlines pay Flight Attendants an hourly rate plus per diem while on the road. Charter flights pay their attendants a salary plus hourly per diem on the road. The per diem is usually between $1.60 to $2.50 an hour, which can add up if you are flying abroad. In some cases, a trip may require you to stay in another city away from home for 10 days or more.

There are a lot of flexible options to being a Flight Attendant. From the choice of base that you will be assigned to the type of flights you will cover, there is something for everybody. There is a saying that aviation is either in your blood or it's not. If you make it through training, there's a great chance it's in your blood. However, the true test comes once you start flying. So, please don't feel that you have to only work for a commercial airline first. Be flexible and open to all opportunities that come your way. You worked hard for this, and your success will only reign on how versatile you are in the profession.

Remember, this is your dream job. You have earned this golden ticket and made lifelong friends along the way. Embrace it and ride this journey. Congratulations on having the courage to achieve your dream of becoming a Flight Attendant.

Come Fly with Me

"Wow, I didn't know all of that was involved with being a Flight Attendant." That's what you're thinking, right? Yes, being a Flight Attendant is no easy task, even though it looks fabulous and glamorous. I promise you that not only will your feet hurt, but your face will hurt, too, from smiling all day. The good news is you will be doing what you love, so it won't matter much to you if your feet are hurting or you're so sleepy you can barely smile. The job is amazing! I have many memories and stories that I can share—from the people I met, the relationships I created, destinations visited, and incidents where I was ready to go home. But to be quite frank, being a Flight Attendant is a great experience, and I am so happy I followed my dream and enjoyed my tenure as one.

If you're wondering how I became The Kissing Flight Attendant, I started a blog focusing on aviation entertainment and tips for a successful flight. I knew I had to have a catchy name, so I prayed about it. The following week at work, I noticed that my passengers would kiss me on my cheek after every flight as they exited the aircraft. Thus, The Kissing Flight Attendant became my name.

Here are a couple of great tips I have shared on my blog:

1. Always keep your cell phone on your body. If there is an emergency evacuation, you can't take any bags with you. So, if your phone is in your purse or briefcase, you'll be in bad shape.

2. Always count how many seats you are away from the closest exit because the plane will be pitch black during an emergency evacuation. Your goal is to get off the plane. This is especially true for children flying alone. I taught this to my children when they started flying by themselves.

In addition to those tips, I will share with you some of my most personal accounts while flying the friendly skies. Some stories are wondrous; others will have you like, "Oh, no, they didn't!" Class is officially over. Now it's time to grab a cool beverage, sit back, get comfy, and enjoy how it goes down in the life of a Flight Attendant--specifically The Kissing Flight Attendant.

A Night in Melia, Mexico

I was selected to be the Flight Attendant aboard the aircraft of the president of the Dominican Republic. He was attending the South America Presidential Summit, where all the presidents of the South American countries would meet to discuss the state of affairs. By far, this is one of the most memorable highlights of my career.

I remember my astonishment when I saw the red carpet rolled out, the band setting up outside in preparation for the president's arrival, and the dogs sniffing luggage. *This is a big deal,* I thought to myself as I prepared the boarding appetizers.

As I turned around to focus on my task, I spotted the Secret Service looking through the plane with the lead flight attendant assisting them. When she started making hand gestures, I went to her aid to see if I could assist. That's when I was informed the Secret Service and 95% of the passengers did not speak English. Well, thank God I knew Spanish and was able to put my gift to great use. You see, being from California, learning Spanish is just as important as learning English. I was taught Spanish as a child growing up and studied Spanish at Howard University. So, in addition to being a Flight Attendant for the flight, I became the in-flight translator. Throughout the trip, everything was amazing. Just as I was becoming more confidant in my translating, the right-hand official to the president said, "You will start dreaming in Spanish." At first, I did not know what that meant, but let me tell you, after three days, it finally happened; I was dreaming in Española.

During the tour's first stop, we were lucky enough to stay in the same hotel as the president we were servicing on the trip. Presidents from other countries stayed there, as well. What a blessing! This rarely happens in charter because the company usually requires the crew to stay close to the Flight Base Office (FBO) in case the plane is needed for another trip. However, this time, we stayed in the best hotel in the city.

After a relaxing day and enjoying a swim with the

president of Chile, we decided to grab a bite to eat. We went to the closest restaurant we could walk to, which was Chili's. We are Americans in Melia, Mexico, and we go to Chili's. Go figure!

After we were seated, there was a flush of rushed energy coming towards us. We did not know whether to sit or run! But then, we noticed the energy was the president's men who had come to the restaurant to eat, too. After a couple hours of catching up and planning our adventures for the following day, we decided to head back to the hotel. We all simultaneously stopped on our way out of the restaurant when we noticed the president's men were our passengers. At the same time, they realized we were their crew and immediately asked us to come over and share a drink with them. After they finished eating, they invited us to have drinks with them at a fancy private restaurant. It was one of the most amazing and adventurous evenings I'd ever had flying as a charter Flight Attendant. I made a personal connection with the president's right-hand man, as we both had children and were closer in age, which left my partner in crime with the president's left-hand man.

After drinks, we went to one of the finest seafood restaurants in Melia, and I tried octopus for the first time. I also had their official drink, tequila with a side of tomato juice. Can I just say it was deliciosa! These men knew how to have fun, and we all left with our bellies full. The party didn't end there, though.

We headed straight to a fabulous lounge where I got to dance off all of the calories of the food and tequila. We toasted to our blessings, talked, and enjoyed being able to relax after hours of flying and working. We also gave each other pet names; I was his Mami, and he was my Papi. The evening ended with me going back to my luxurious hotel room. Filling my bath with warm water and expensive sea salts, compliments of the hotel. I thanked God for this blessing. I never dreamed I would ever be enjoying life with dignitaries as a Flight Attendant. This is what manifesting miracles looks like! This is what believing in yourself looks like! In that moment, I was fully present and appreciative of sitting in my dream job— happy, healthy, and at home in my purpose. How many of you want this? Can you give yourself permission to feel what your dreams look like? Being a Flight Attendant gives you permission to just be, and for that, I was immensely grateful.

The next day, we left Melia and went to Bogota, Columbia. Unfortunately, the crew did not get to stay in the same hotel as the presidents, but I still managed to enjoy my new Papi during brief moments. When it was all said and done, Papi and I managed to spend two weeks together. The craziest thing about our relationship was that neither of us was fluent in the other's language, but our hearts provided all the communication we needed. Our time together was beautiful to experience, and he was such a gentleman. Whenever I visited the Dominican Republic, he would come to the hotel to have lunch with me and take me around sightseeing. Because of his position, the hotel staff would ensure he and I had everything we needed. Talk about 5-star service! I will never forget this time because I had an opportunity to be around influential men and women making decisions for a nation.

I'm sharing this story to confirm to someone that special friendships can appear in one of the craziest places or when least expected. It doesn't always have to manifest into something bigger; sometimes, it's the little moments shared that mean the most to us. So, if you happen to find it on the road, embrace it and enjoy being loved by someone who doesn't want or need anything from you but a moment of your time and attention.

Stuck in
The Dominican Republic

Imagine being the Flight Attendant to the incomparable Jennifer Lopez, aka JLo. I remember servicing as a Flight Attendant on the charter flight for Ms. Lopez's tour. It was by far the craziest music tour experience ever.

The plane in Venezuela broke down, and we were stranded there for days, paying well over $50 per meal. I'm talking burger and fries. Then the charter company sent another plane and crew to get Ms. Lopez crew to their next destination while we waited in Venezuela for the plane to be repaired. Once the aircraft in Venezuela was fixed, we all prepared to reconnect with Ms. Lopez in Barcelona, Spain, to continue the tour with her. Or so we thought. As I told you, being a Flight Attendant, you must be flexible and quickly adapt to change. That includes your flight plans. After a few hours and a good burger, we were told we would have to fly out the next day to the Dominican Republic for the president to use the plane for his trip with another crew. Seven whole days in the Dominican Republic! What was a woman to do? I couldn't call Papi because he was on the road with the president. What to do?

We had the best time of our lives! We went to the casinos, bars, toured the city, and lounged by the pool. We met more people, and it was there that I got my first sunburn. What the hell? Black people do get sunburned! That sunburn was the worst ever—the pain, peeling skin, and blisters! I was thankful my coworkers were able to tell me what to do and how to heal my skin. Our time together gave us the opportunity to get to know each other better as a crew and trust each other more. We didn't know all of the life-changing moments we would experience collectively and individually on this particular trip. All things happen for a reason; the universe knew what it was doing by having us stuck together in the DR for a week.

This story is an example of why being flexible is a

must as a Flight Attendant. Things are subject to change when you least expect them. When they do, your response should be a smile and a "let's make it happen" attitude.

Farewell Fortaleza, Brazil

This story is another experience I had while servicing Jennifer Lopez on her South American Tour. We had just left Rio De Janeiro on our way to the last stop of the tour in Fortaleza, Brazil. By now, exhaustion was everyone's friend. The tour had taken a major toll on her team and the flight crew, as well. Everyone except me experienced some form of a mental breakdown. As a motivator, I was there to cheer everyone on, and I do mean everyone. I never thought there would be so much drama with a stage crew dancer, band, etc. They had a new story after every show. You see, as a Flight Attendant, you will hear the most private conversations while working. Like a beautiful butterfly on the wall, I was there, but they were not paying attention to me.

Being away from family for almost a month was rough for some people. Once we landed in Fortaleza, Brazil, everyone just wanted to rest. Our second night there, it was my turn to face having a mental breakdown. Mine did not pertain to the tour, though. Mine had to do with my family. I remember this as if it was yesterday.

I had received an email message from my niece, Kenecia, telling me that I needed to call home immediately. It was late. We had just got back from walking around the city, enjoying the arts and crafts and nightlife. I wondered if it was an actual emergency or did she just miss me and want to talk? When you are on the road that long, you never know what to expect when you call back home.

Well, when I called home this time, I was greeted with the news that my brother, Duvall Lamont Cross, had passed away. Talk about shocked and heartbroken! What was I supposed to do now? I couldn't just hop back on the plane and instruct the pilot to fly me home. This is one of the disadvantages of being a Flight Attendant. In the case of a family emergency, especially charter flying, you can't just book a flight and head home. You are at work and expected to work until the end of the assignment. But thank God for having a crew that stepped in as family and helped me work through the pain and smile through the tears. The Lead Flight Attendant Michelle, aka T1, and Senior Jamie, one of the best pilots I have ever worked with, created a bouquet for me from flowers they had picked from the road. How sweet was that? Michelle supported me the night we went back to work and helped me get through the final leg of the trip. At this point, we had also become like family with the passengers. So, once they found out why I was not my cheerful self, they supported me, as well, and together, we all got through that final long flight until we landed back home and back to reality.

I shared this story to remind you that life happens whether you are at home or away. Time waits for no one. Always let your family know you love them before leaving home because you never know if you will make it back or if they will be there when you return.

Cleveland Rocks

First of all, let me mention that Cleveland is one of the most fun-loving and coldest cities I have ever been to in America. This story is about my encounter with an NBA Assistant Coach who insisted on taking your girl out. I mean, every city we traveled to, he was persistent with his offer. It wasn't until we were in Cleveland that I finally decided to accept his offer to take me out. We went to an underground fancy restaurant for food and drinks.

While at dinner, he kept insisting that I finish my drink. I wondered to myself what was the rush. I mean, it was a known fact that restaurants stayed open past their business hours to accommodate NBA players and their leadership. So, I was in no rush to leave.

I excused myself to go to the bathroom, hoping he would back off rushing me to hurry up with my beverage. But when I returned, he continued encouraging me to finish my drink. Since it was getting late, I went ahead and finished my drink. As we continued to talk, I started to feel weird. Never in my mind did I think he had drugged me. I chalked it up as the liquor, the time, and jetlag. When I told him that I needed to go back to my hotel room, he played to be the perfect gentleman and escorted me there. As we walked, I kept dropping the keys and even dropped my cash. He gave me the keys but kept the money.

After we got to my room, he helped me take off my clothes and get into bed. I remember him leaving four hours later, but I could not get up to walk him to the door. My body was stuck to the bed. I knew we had wild and adventurous sex; it was indeed a night to remember. However, when I tried to get up, I experienced a soreness over my whole body that felt different. I had no energy, and my whole body was stiff and stuck in that one position. Strange!

I laid there hoping that if I got more sleep, I would wake up feeling refreshed. When I eventually woke up, I could move, but my movements were slower than usual. With a job to do, I pulled myself together. It was time to get up, get with my daily routine, and prepare for work later that evening after the game.

Later that evening, it was like my body rebirthed what happened the night before; I mentally relived that experience in pieces. By the end of the week, I knew exactly why he wanted me to finish my drink and what happened after leaving the restaurant. If I can be transparent, I have to say that I do not regret what happened because I had every intention of having sex with him. However, I did not expect him to drug me to get what we both wanted. After that experience, I never left my drink unattended, and if I had to, I would order a new one.

I shared this story to warn you to be careful when you are traveling or just hanging out. There are people out there who will go to the extreme to get what they want. This story is not an isolated case, so be careful when you're on the road. Let one of your crew members know where you are at all times. Sadly, there are many stories of people in this profession being stalked and even killed while on a layover.

I Will Hold You, Lord Stanley

Now this story is about another sports crew—the NHL. However, I experienced a new thing this time. If you haven't already noticed, it goes down on the road! This story is a continuation of the one I mentioned in my last book, *The Message 108*. In that story, I was a cheerleader and motivator; this is not that. This is the following night—different player, different motivation.

I worked on the flight with the Chicago Blackhawks when they won the Stanley Cup in 2010 against the Philadelphia Flyers. After the win, the players got on the plane, and of course, that's when the official party began. There was a lot of champagne drinking out of the Lord

Stanley Cup and players taking pictures with the shiny trophy. Players started getting texts informing them that parties were being thrown for them, the first one being at the hotel where we would be staying. We were so happy when they invited our crew to celebrate with them.

When we landed in Chicago, fire trucks were lined up on the runway to give the players a celebratory rain shower welcoming them home with the Lord Stanley Championship Cup. Once the door of the aircraft opened, you could hear the fans cheering. It was incredible! We could not wait to get to the hotel and change clothes to go to the party. Then we heard there was a second party popping off, too. It was on!

We all rushed to the hotel, changed clothes, and started party hopping! After barely making it to the party in the hotel, we hopped into the limo with the coaching staff to go to the team's celebration being held in the city. I had a ball! One of the players called me over to look at the sea of fans celebrating outside the club's window. I felt so special that we were their guests. It was always like that with our clients; they would invite us to everything and treat us like we were the celebrities.

What was also amazing about this trip is I got to experience my first threesome! Okay, you can pick your lip up now. Yes, baby! I don't know about you, but I always had a thing for athletes, they have amazing bodies, and I could not pass up the opportunity to experience them for myself. Babbyyyyy! If you get lucky enough to work on a charter with any sports team, one thing you should know is that the airplane is the players' locker room. Coaches go over plays, and clothes are changed right there in the aisle. It is a beautiful sight, I promise you. Being on the road gets lonely sometimes, and we all need a little love. So, please don't judge me is all I can say! Now back to the story.

After looking out the window, we were escorted to the back door, where a black sedan was waiting for us. The player we were with asked us to come to his house and make it do what it do. I spoke to my friend and admitted I had never done a threesome before. She explained what would happen and took control over the situation, so I let my guard down and got comfortable.

Once we got into the sedan, she read him the rules to let him know how it was going down if he wanted us to play. We agreed to his request, and the three of us proceeded to the condominium. As we pulled up to the condo, I remember thinking how beautiful the Chicago building looked.

As we approached the condo, the doorman opened the door to the sedan and greeted us. Once we made it to his floor and he opened the front door, I could not believe I was in this man's house and had agreed to "make it do what it do." I had to tell myself to take deep breaths.

The lights were dimmed, and the mood was set. It was clear we were not there to play Uno and eat chips. Then, so seductively like a scene out of a movie, he opened the door, and the smell of his cologne had me ready to make "magic." My friend gave him the final rules, and without another word, we made it do exactly what it was supposed to do! I have no regrets. That was a liberating moment for me, and it felt good to try something new.

I shared this story to remind you that if you are open to new experiences, moments, and adventures, being a Flight Attendant will give you every opportunity to pursue them. Now, I know I shared different kinds of stories with you, and by no means am I encouraging you to sleep with or fall in love with your passengers. But don't be afraid to live. The road gets lonely, and at times, a strong arm will provide the comfort you need to get you through. Some people indulge in alcohol while others turn to drugs, but everyone has a vice that provides them an escape, even if only temporary. Whatever you decide, be careful, enjoy life, and hold on to your stories as learning lessons of life and how it is what you make it.

White House Down

This story involves being on the road with the White House Press Corps and the importance of being flexible and a leader. I was serving as the Lead on this particular trip with President Obama. Our flights would usually get to the city an hour or two after the president's plane arrived. I remember this trip very well, as it impacted our nation in a significant way.

We were overnighting in Florida, and the evening news reported a movie theater shooting in another city. As the lead Flight Attendant, I received a phone call that President Obama was leaving early the following morning and would hold a press conference at the FBO. Little did I know I would play a major part in the press conference. Once again, I had the task of communicating our jet's movements and schedule with the Secret Service. I also was responsible for making sure my passengers, the White House Press Corps, had what they needed on the plane to complete their interviews for the morning shows. Once that was done, I had to get the logistics of getting the flight crew securely into the FBO due to the heightened security. Talk about an adrenaline rush! This was one of those things that require you to take the lead as a Flight Attendant because you never know what will happen when working these types of high-security flights.

Although I would fly all over America following President Obama, I never saw him—only his plane leaving before ours. This time, I was able to see him during his press conference and be a part of this defining moment in our country. I learned life is precious. One minute, everything is on schedule, and the next minute, it's an emergency.

I share this story to let you know once again that it gets real on the road, and you have to step up whether you're ready or not because your country and crew will be depending on you.

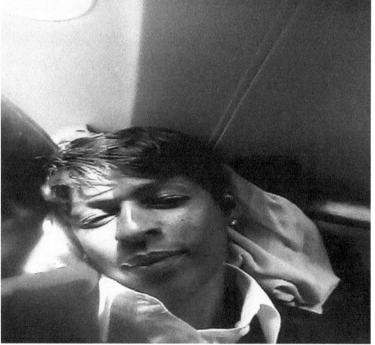

Thank You for Traveling Flight 108

Congratulations, and thank you for flying Flight 108! Having read this book, I hope you feel more empowered and educated on pursuing and securing your wings. There are a lot of organizations and Flight Attendants that are ready to mentor and guide you through the process. As you have read, the process is highly intense. However, I know you are a fighter and committed to achieving your goals.

The good news is we are coming out of the pandemic, which means there are a lot of opportunities opening for

Flight Attendants. Some airlines furloughed or terminated Flight Attendants because of low passenger bookings, but things are turning around. So, be encouraged because airlines are going to start hiring again. They need to refill those positions and get some new butts in those jump seats. There will always be some major event that will cause airlines to let go or hire Flight Attendants. Knowing this, start applying now so once things ramp up, you are not facing heavy competition. Rest assured, the need for Flight Attendants will outlive these times. If you are ready to travel and enjoy life from the clouds, it's time to live your dreams.

It has been my honor to serve as your Instructor as we examined the ins and outs of becoming a Flight Attendant. I wanted this book not to just read like a training manual, but a point of reference with a touch of my personal experience. I want you to fully understand what you will be facing. Many people see the uniform and assume it's a life of happiness while in the friendly skies, but we all know the saying, "To whom much is given, much is required." Being a Flight Attendant is great, but the sacrifice and strain will cost you so much. But as long as you remember your *why*, you will soar and find the balance needed to live out your dreams while having the life you desire.

I wish you much success on your journey and can't wait to hear about you receiving your wings. If you require my support, please feel free to contact me via my website: https://www.expectamiracle108.com/. As your coach and Angel in aviation, it has been an incredible journey. Now it's time to head to the hotel and relax.

Thank you for traveling Flight 108. Again, I'm Charlotte Crumley Arrington, The Kissing Flight Attendant. Signing off! Muah! Bye Bye! ☺

XOXOX,

Charlotte Crumley Arrington

Motivational Speaker, Author, and Trainer

Glossary

Flight Attendants and other airline employees speak a different "language." Many of the everyday terms they use are unique to the airline business. Knowing these terms before you apply will be very helpful.

A

"A" Flight Attendant
The flight attendant assigned to work the senior position on a flight. Also referred to as "Lead" or "Senior" flight attendant or "Purser" (on international flights). Warrants additional pay.

Aerophobia
The fear of flying.

AFA–CWA
Abbreviation for Association of Flight Attendants, the largest flight attendant labor union in the U.S.

Air Rage

A phenomenon whereby passengers vent their frustrations (sometimes violently) on crewmembers during a flight due to perceived inadequacies in airline service.

Aircraft Forward

Section in the forward part of an aircraft.

Aircraft Fuselage

The complete central structure of an aircraft to which wings, tail surfaces, and engines are attached. Includes entire cabin and cockpit areas.

Aircraft Left

Refers to the left interior portion of an aircraft.

Aircraft Right

Refers to the right interior portion of an aircraft.

Airline Deregulation

Refers to the Airline Deregulation Act of 1978, which removed the governmental authority to regulate airfares and airline route structures. In the current deregulated environment, airlines can fly anywhere and charge any price they desire.

Airport Code

A unique 3-letter airport identification code (e.g., BOS = Boston's Logan Airport). Every airport has an airport code, also referred to as an "Airport Identifier."

Alternate Airport

The airport to which an aircraft diverts when it cannot land at its destination airport due to weather or other problems. See also "Divert."

A-Scale

An airline's maximum contractual pay scale.

B

Background Check

A 5 to 10-year check by an employer of an applicant's history. Can include checks on work, education, family, medical, and criminal or civil offense history.

Base Rate

The basic hourly rate a crewmember is paid. Excludes per diem and other forms of incentive pay.

Beverage Cart

A wheeled cart onboard an aircraft, which flight attendants

use for beverage and meal service. Also called a "meal cart." Collapses for quick stowage in the galley area.

Bid Closing Date
A published date and time marking the end of the bidding period.

Bid Opening Date
A published date and time marking the beginning of the bidding period. Flight attendants may bid on monthly lines, vacations, and domiciles.

Bid Package
A published listing of all trip pairings and lines of time available for a specific period, usually one month.

Bid Sharing
A practice offered at some airlines in which two flight attendants may share or split the same line of time.

Bid
Flight attendants bid on monthly lines, vacations, and domiciles. Bid results are awarded based on relative seniority.

Block Time

Also known as "Block-to-Block" time or "Hard Time," this is the actual time an aircraft leaves the blocks and pushes back from the gate to the time it arrives (and is blocked in) at its destination's gate.

Boarding

The term used to describe the process of passengers getting on an aircraft, stowing their carry-on articles, and taking their assigned seats.

Briefing

A procedure initiated by an individual in charge of a group during which specific items of responsibility are reviewed and delegated. Captains and senior flight attendants initiate crew briefings following every crew change. Briefings can also cover irregular operations, emergency procedures, medical emergencies, etc.

B-Scale

A second-tier pay scale within an airline.

Buddy Bidding

A system that allows 2 flight attendants to bid the identical schedule.

Buddy Pass

A reduced rate, space-available pass that allows a friend or family member to travel on an airline. Most airlines allow a specified number of buddy passes for each employee per year. Typical cost is 50 to 90% off the full coach fare. Also referred to as a "Companion Pass."

Bulkhead Seat

The seat or seats located directly behind the partition separating various cabins of an aircraft.

Business Class

A premium service offered on most international flights with 2 or 3 classes of service. Amenities may include larger seats, complimentary cocktails, and upgraded meal service.

C

Cabin Crew

The flight attendants assigned to work a specific flight, trip, or series of trips.

Captain

The pilot in command of an aircraft who is responsible for the safe operation of the flight.

Charter Flight

A non-scheduled flight, often exclusively booked by a sports team, band, or vacation group. Routes may be on the airline's regular route system or "offline" to a city not served by the airline.

Cleaners

The ground personnel that cleans an aircraft between legs. At some airlines, these individuals are members of the same union as mechanics and are also used for other duties such as aircraft pushback. Also called "Utility Crew."

Coach

The largest and usually the most basic class of service on an aircraft. Some aircraft have only a coach class of service, while on others, coach may be a part of a 2 or 3 class configuration.

Cockpit Crew

The individuals responsible for piloting an aircraft. Normally a 2 or 3-pilot crew consisting of a captain, first officer, and second officer (if applicable). Long international flights may carry 2 complete cockpit crews.

Commute

The process of commuting by air to a given domicile.

Commuter Airline
Small airlines that are part of the regional airline category. Some are affiliated with major airlines and act as feeders to the mainline routes.

Commuter
An individual who commutes by air to a given domicile.

Configuration
Refers to the class(es) of service onboard an aircraft: First class, Business class, Coach class, etc.

Contract Negotiations
The formal talks between an airline and elected representatives of a labor group that allows for the establishment (or renewal) of a labor contract. The working agreement covers pay, benefits, union security, seniority, scheduling, work rules, vacations, sick time, handling grievances (complaints), etc.

Contractual Work Rules
The airline-specific rules published in a labor contract that govern maximum flight hours, on-duty time, days worked, scheduling procedures, etc. Also referred to as "Work Rules."

Crash Pad

Term used by commuters to refer to their "home away from home." Also referred to as a "Commuter Apartment." Usually shared by several commuters to reduce costs.

Crew Legalities

A measure of whether or not a crewmember is abiding by the section of the labor contract that governs hours flown, rest periods, and on-duty times.

Crew Schedulers

The group of individuals responsible for making sure routine and non-routine flights depart on time with a sufficient number of crewmembers.

D

Date of Hire

The date a flight attendant begins or graduates from training. Date of hire establishes a seniority number within an airline.

Deadhead Time

The pay time associated with a deadhead flight. See "Claim Time."

Deadhead

The process of traveling on an aircraft as a passenger while on duty (often in uniform). Flight attendants frequently deadhead to reposition for flight segments originating from other cities. Usage: "I had to deadhead to Boston."

Defibrillator

A medical device carried on an aircraft that allows flight attendants to treat victims of cardiac arrest.

Delay

Time period during which an aircraft is held before it is allowed to depart. Delays may be caused by maintenance (mechanical problems), air traffic, weather, connecting passengers, weight and balance, etc.

Deplaning

The term used to describe the process of passengers getting off an aircraft once it has arrived at the gate and the seatbelt sign has been turned off by the captain.

Direct Flight

A single flight number that makes 1 or more stops before reaching its final destination. Many people confuse "direct" flights with "non-stop" flights.

Divert

A procedure where pilots elect to land at an airport other than the airport of the intended destination. This can be due to adverse weather, a medical emergency, a closed runway, etc.

Domicile

The city and associated airport a flight attendant is assigned to. The domicile is where all trips begin and end. Also referred to as "Base" or "Crew Base."

Door Arming

The procedure for preparing an aircraft door so its associated escape slide will deploy upon opening.

Door Slide

A device used to escape quickly from an aircraft during an emergency evacuation.

Duty Time

The period of time a crewmember is on duty. Includes the period from check-in to off-duty time.

E

Emergency Exits
Specified doors and windows on an aircraft used during an emergency evacuation.

ETA
Abbreviation for "Estimated Time of Arrival." Also referred to as "Arrival Time."

ETD
Abbreviation for "Estimated Time of Departure." Also referred to as "Departure Time."

Evacuation
An emergency procedure that allows the rapid removal of passengers and crew from an aircraft using all suitable exits, including slides and over-wing exits. Also referred to as a "Passenger Evacuation."

Extended Sick Leave
An extended period of time during which a flight attendant is unable to work due to serious illness.

Extra Section

An additional flight added to a scheduled destination to accommodate additional passengers. Extra sections are common during peak travel periods (especially during the holidays to popular destinations).

F

F/A

Abbreviation for flight attendant.

F/A Emergency Manual

A manual required by the FAA to be personally carried at all times by every on-duty flight attendant. Also called an "Emergency Procedures Manual," this manual governs all normal and emergency flight attendant procedures.

F/A Jumpseat

A fold-down seat used by flight attendants during taxi, take-off, and turbulence. Non-working flight attendants can ride the jumpseat on heavily-booked flights.

Ferry Flight

A repositioning flight flown with no revenue passengers onboard. Usually flown by pilots only, but flight attendants are sometimes onboard, as well.

FFDO

Abbreviation for "Federal Flight Deck Officer." A designated pilot who is armed in order to defend the cockpit against terrorist attacks and air piracy. An FFDO may be working or deadheading.

Firearm Authorization

A notification slip presented to the senior flight attendant that identifies passengers carrying authorized firearms (e.g., federal marshals and secret service members). The firearm authorization slip identifies the armed passenger (and accompanied prisoner, if applicable) by seat number and must be presented to the captain.

First Class

The highest class of service onboard an aircraft. Amenities may include larger seats, complimentary cocktails, and upgraded meal service.

First Officer

Second-in-command pilot on an aircraft. Also referred to as a "Copilot."

Flight Attendant

A person responsible for the safety and comfort of all passengers during a flight.

Flight Hour Option

A bid position offered by some airlines that allows a flight attendant to fly less or more than a normal monthly line of time.

Flight Hours

Total number of hours flown in any given period used for pay computation.

Flight Miles

Miles flown in any given period used for pay computation at some airlines. One trip equals 243 miles.

Flight Time

Sometimes known as "Airtime," this is the time allowed from takeoff to touchdown for a specific flight. Flight time is block time less taxi time and gives flight attendants an idea of how much time they will have to provide in-flight service.

FOB

Fuel on board.

Full Month

A term used to refer to the maximization of flight hours for any given month.

Furlough

A layoff of an airline employee due to financial difficulties, labor union strikes, etc.

G

Galley

The area inside an aircraft where flight attendants prepare meals and beverages.

Gate

The airport boarding area at an airport terminal for a specific flight number.

Get Your Time In

Refers to the practice of maximizing flight hours in order to get a "Full Month."

H

Hijacking

A militaristic act of aggression by a passenger onboard an aircraft whereby crewmembers and other passengers are taken hostage until the hijacker's demands are met.

Hub

An airport through which the majority of an airline's traffic passes to meet connecting flights. Many airlines have multiple hubs.

I

Illegal

A term used to describe a crewmember who can no longer legally continue to work due to a violation of scheduling restrictions in the labor contract. For example, a crewmember who exceeds the 16-hour daily maximum on-duty period becomes illegal.

Initial Training

Training that all new hires must complete. Also referred to as "New-Hire Training."

Instructor

An individual who conducts initial and recurrent flight attendant training classes. Also referred to as a "Trainer."

Interline Discounts

Travel industry discounts available to airline crewmembers.

International Flight

A flight that departs a domestic location and lands at an international destination.

Interviewer

An individual who conducts interviews with flight attendant applicants.

J

Jetway

The passageway between the gate area and an aircraft that allows passengers to board and deplane.

Junior

A term used as a measure of one's relative seniority at an airline or any given base, e.g., "How junior are you?" Also used to describe the seniority of a specific flight attendant domicile. ("Is that a junior base?")

L

Labor Contract

An official document negotiated between labor and management that covers pay, benefits, union security, seniority, scheduling, work rules, vacation, sick time, grievances, etc. Also called a "Working Agreement."

Labor Union

A body of members and elected representatives that seek to negotiate labor contracts and handle job disputes. They also actively represent members in the media and fight battles in the political arena.

Layover

A period of time a crewmember is scheduled to remain at a specified location, e.g., a 2-hour layover in PIT. Extended layovers are termed "RON" for "Remain Overnight."

Leave of Absence

A period of time granted by an airline for a flight attendant to pursue other interests or needs before returning to work. Types of leaves include education, military, and parental leave. Seniority continues to accrue during most leaves.

Leg

A single flight from one departure point to one destination point. A leg includes one takeoff and one landing.

Line of Time

A monthly schedule.

Lineholder

A crewmember with sufficient seniority to fly (or hold) a regular line of time. Also referred to as a "Blockholder."

Line Sharing

A system that allows 2 flight attendants to split a monthly line of time.

LOD/O

Acronym for "Language of Destination/Origin." A flight attendant who is assigned to an international trip as a second language speaker.

M

MedLink

A medical agency used by some airlines that provides in-flight personnel direct communication with a physician during medical emergencies.

Military Time

The time on a 24-hour clock used by airlines and crewmember's industry-wide in reading trip pairings. Also referred to as "24-hour clock time."

Minimum Guarantee

Minimum number of hours to be paid in a given month regardless of the number of hours flown. Applies to reserves only.

Monthly Projection

Projected number of flight hours at the end of the current month based on projected flying activity.

N

Narrow Body

An aircraft with a single aisle with seats on either side of the aisle.

National Airline

An airline with between $100 million and $1 billion annual operating revenue.

New-Hire

A flight attendant who has just completed initial training. Flight attendants are usually classified as new hires during the first six months of employment.

No Contact

A flight attendant infraction resulting from a crew scheduler being unable to reach a flight attendant for a trip assignment. Usually applies to reserves only.

Non-Rev

Abbreviation for "Non-Revenue," a term used to describe airline employees who travel using space-available passes. Also referred to as "Space-A travel." *Usage: "Are you a non-rev passenger?" or "Are you flying non-rev?"*

Non-Stop Flight

A single flight number with one takeoff and one landing to reach its destination. See also "Direct Flight."

O

On-Call

A period of time during which a reserve flight attendant may be assigned a trip.

On-Duty

The period of time a flight attendant is "working," from check-in time until going off-duty. Reserves also use this term in reference to being on-call.

Open Time
Uncovered trips available for bid by lineholders. Can also be assigned to reserves.

Out-and-In
A one-day trip that flies to one destination and returns. Also referred to as a "Turnaround."

Out-of-Time
A situation in which a flight attendant reaches the maximum time ceiling (i.e., flight hour limit) and is no longer legal to fly. Usually applies to being "Out of Time" for the month.

Overwater Flight
A flight that exceeds 50 nautical miles from the coastline requiring an emergency life vest and raft demo. See also "Transoceanic Flight."

Overhead Bin
Stowage area above the passenger seats. Carry-on bags are required to fit into these bins. Also referred to as an "Overhead Compartment."

P

Pass Privileges
Rules and regulations published by each airline that provide specific guidance on non-revenue travel.

Passenger Count
The final count of passengers delivered by the senior flight attendant.

Pay Time
This is the time used for pay purposes.

Per Diem
Latin for "by the day." Refers to the hourly rate paid to flight attendants for meal expenses while on duty.

Picket Line
A line of workers carrying signs during labor negotiations expressing dissatisfaction with their airline. Picket lines may be formed for information purposes only. Picket lines may also be formed during a work stoppage or just before a union's implementation of "CHAOS." See "Strike," "CHAOS," "Labor Contract," Labor Union."

Pre-board

A procedure during which passengers with small children and those needing assistance (e.g., wheelchair passengers) are boarded before regular passengers. These individuals are also referred to as "Pre-boards."

Pre-flight

The period of time before passenger boarding during which emergency equipment is checked, briefings are completed, catering supplies are checked, etc.

Probationary Period

A period of time, usually lasting from 6 to 12 months, during which a new hire's performance is evaluated by an airline. Also referred to as "Probation" or "Being on Probation."

PSR

Abbreviation for "Passenger Service Agent." The person responsible for passengers from the time they check-in (at the gate) until the aircraft's cabin door is closed. Duties include passenger check-in, baggage checking, and assistance with passengers in wheelchairs. Also responsible for confirming that fuel quantity and passenger count are correct before entry door is closed. Also referred to as a "Ticket Agent" or "Agent."

PSU

Abbreviation for "Passenger Service Unit." A unit above each row of passenger seats that houses individual passenger oxygen units, reading lights, flight attendant call buttons, etc.

Pushback

The process of moving an aircraft backwards from the gate, which is accomplished by coordination between the pilots and ground maintenance crew.

Q

Quick Call

A trip assigned to a reserve lineholder, which requires reporting to the flight as soon as possible.

R

Ramp Workers

Maintenance personnel, cleaners, fuelers, caterers, etc.

Ramp

The area around an aircraft where ground personnel performs their duties. This includes maintenance, baggage handling, catering, fueling, etc.

Reach Test

A test instituted by several airlines to determine whether a flight attendant applicant will be tall enough to perform the duties required for the job.

Recall

The action of calling back a furloughed worker to the job.

Recurrent Training

Annual refresher training required by the FAA to be completed by all flight attendants.

Red-eye

A flight, typically from the West Coast, that departs late in the evening and flies eastbound all night to the destination airport.

Regional Airline

An airline with less than $100 million in annual operating revenue. Includes commuter airlines.

Registered Alien

A person who has the legal right to accept employment in the United States. Registered aliens must possess what is called a "Green Card."

Regular Line of Time

A unique schedule that features specific trip pairings typically over a 4-week period. Also referred to as a "Block" or "Pattern."

Rejected Takeoff

A sudden, unexpected stop of an aircraft (on the runway) following the takeoff roll due to a mechanical issue or another type of problem. Also referred to as an "Aborted Takeoff."

Report Time

The time you are required to be at the airport for check-in.

Reservationist

An airline representative who books flights and assists passengers with reservation and/or ticket problems.

Reserve

A crewmember with insufficient seniority to hold a regular line of time. A reserve must fly a reserve line of time, which features no assigned trips and no set schedule other than days off.

Reserve Line of Time

A schedule that features no assigned trips and no set schedule other than days off.

S

Scab

A crewmember who crosses a picket line and continues to work during a strike or other type of work stoppage.

Second Officer

Third-in-command of an aircraft. Normally a non-flying position. Also referred to as a "Flight Engineer."

Senior

A term used as a measure of one's relative seniority at an airline or any given base, e.g., "How senior are you?" Also used to describe the seniority of a specific flight attendant domicile. ("Is that a senior base?")

Seniority List

A list published by an airline listing the seniority number of every employed flight attendant.

Seniority Number

A unique number assigned to each flight attendant based

Charlotte Crumley Arrington

on date of hire. See also "Date of Hire."

Seniority
A numerical ranking system (based on date of hire) used by the airlines to determine awards of line positions, vacations, domiciles, etc.

Show Time
See "Check-in Time."

Sick Time
Accrued time (in a sick bank) that is required to receive paid sick days.

Sterile Cockpit
The time during the critical phase of flight when the cockpit door must be locked and flight attendants are restricted from entering (except in an emergency). A sterile cockpit is required when an aircraft is below 10,000 feet and includes taxi, takeoff, and landing.

Stewardess
Original term used to describe a flight attendant before the 70s.

Strike

Legal work stoppage by labor due to an inability to reach a labor contract agreement with management.

Supervisor

A flight attendant manager who is directly responsible for flight attendants at a given domicile.

T

Taxi

The act of moving an aircraft on the ground under its own power.

Termination

Usually refers to the last flight of the day for a specific aircraft but can also refer to the last flight of the day for a crew.

Terminator

An aircraft that is finished flying on a given day upon arrival at its destination.

Transcontinental Flight

A flight that travels non-stop across the country, usually from coast to coast.

Transoceanic Flight
A flight that travels across the Atlantic or Pacific Oceans to reach its destination.

Trip Check-in
The time a flight attendant is required to check-in for an assigned trip. Usually at least one hour before departure, depending on the airline.

Trip Pairing
A series of flight numbers that comprise a trip. Also simply called a "Trip."

Tuff Cuffs
A handcuff restraining device carried onboard an aircraft used by flight attendants to restrain unruly passengers.

Turbulence
Irregular motion of the atmosphere, causing a rough ride on an aircraft. Also referred to as "Air Turbulence."

U

Unaccompanied Minor
An underage child traveling alone on an airplane.

Union Dues
Monthly payment required to maintain individual labor union membership in good standing.

V

Van Time
The time the crew is expected to meet in the hotel lobby after a RON. Also called "Limo Time" or "Pickup Time."

W

Weight and Balance
Series of computations, usually automated and sent via computer to the cockpit. Includes gross aircraft weight, passenger and cargo weight, optimum runway, wing flap settings, etc.

Wide Body
An aircraft with two aisles with rows of seats in the center of the two aisles and on each side.

Write-up
A logbook entry that describes a defect or discrepancy on an aircraft that needs maintenance. Usually, these items are entered by pilots in the cockpit logbook, but there is also a

Charlotte Crumley Arrington

cabin logbook for flight attendant write-ups in some instances.

References

Airline Career. Flight Attendant Dictionary
https://airlinecareer.com/tests/flight-attendant-dictionary/
(retrieved on August 15, 2021)

AvStop.com — History of the flight attendant at History of the Flight Attendant (avstop.com) (retrieved August 7, 2021)

Bureau of Labor Statistics, U.S. Department of Labor, Occupational Outlook Handbook, Flight Attendants at https://www.bls.gov/ooh/transportation-and-material-moving/flight-attendants.htm (retrieved August 07, 2021)

The Travel Academy, Flight Attendants Requirements at https://thetravelacademy.com/travel-careers/flight-attendant-school/flight-attendant-requirements-qualifications#southwest_flight_attendant_guidelines (retrieved on August 5, 2021)

Flight Attendant Certificate of Demonstrated Proficiency at https://www.faa.gov/other_visit/aviation_industry/airline_operators/airline_safety/info/all_infos/media/2008/facert.pdf (retrieved on August 15, 2021)

Charlotte Crumley Arrington

Stratos Jet Charter, Inc., What is a Charter Flight?
https://www.stratosjets.com/faq/what-is-a-charter-flight/
(retrieved on August 2, 2021)

About the Author

Charlotte Crumley Arrington is A Businesswoman, Motivational Speaker, Author, and Life Coach. Charlotte is a graduate of Howard University School of Communications in Washington DC. And a Member of one of the Devine 9, Zeta Phi Beta Sorority Inc. Charlotte is also a member of Women's Empower Network for women in Sciences. Charlotte is very passionate about motivating people to do what God has called them to do and teaching them the tangible skills to make it happen. Charlotte's diverse background and life experiences have prepared her for this fulfilling opportunity to motivate and coach with purpose. Charlotte has had the unique opportunity to travel worldwide, encouraging people to believe in the beauty of their dreams. Charlotte has used her Motivating and Speaking gifts thousands of feet in the air amongst some of the world's most influential people. Charlotte's first dream had always been to become a Flight Attendant, and it wasn't long before that dream came true. She became a first-class Flight Attendant with American Airlines and continued with Swift Aviation, a private charter airline, as a Lead Flight Attendant. While working with the private charter airline, Charlotte served the White House Press Corps, NBA, NHL, MLB, MLS, A-list celebrities, Presidents, and Dignitaries of other countries.

Charlotte also has a funny bone, which led to her being the opening act for several comedy shows starring Steve Harvey, Dave Chappelle, and Tommy Davidson. Charlotte has had the distinct honor of serving as the keynote speaker for an American Airlines Flight Attendant graduation and events at her Alma Mater, Howard University in Washington DC.

Charlotte gets her gift honestly as she comes from a family of Believers. Charlotte's grandfather, Reverend Willis Brown, Sr., is the founder of Gethsemane Baptist Church in Charleston, South Carolina, which has been in her family for 100 years. The church is now pastored by her first cousin, Reverend Herbert Harvey.

Charlotte was born in Honolulu, Hawaii, and raised in San Diego, California, by two amazing parents—

Barbara and Jesse Crumley. She has a brother, Duvall, and a sister, Latarsha. During her time at Howard, Charlotte married recording artist Joe Tex, Jr. and is the mother of three phenomenal adult children—Joseph, Jessica, and Brian.

Charlotte is also a Trainer for a Bio-Marketing firm and is now focusing on her mission, passion, and purpose of motivating people to reach their highest potential and follow their dreams— just as she is doing, too. Her mission is for people to believe in the beauty of their dreams, manifest their heart's desires, and to expect a miracle.

Other Books by Ms. Crumley-Arrington

Greatness isn't simply a fleeting thought. It has to be manifested. However, manifestation doesn't take place without ACTION, and action begins with YOU.

From debut author Charlotte Crumley Arrington, *The Message 108* is an explosive playbook for readers who not only want to see the desires of their hearts come true, but they refuse to lose! As you flip through the pages of *The Message 108* ("108" being a divine number signifying the time is now), let Charlotte serve as your coach, providing you with creative strategies highlighting tangible skills that produce winning results. Everything you've been working, praying, and training for is set to become your reality. All you need are the right plays to make it happen. Every page, every encouraging word, and every strategy outlined is designed to lead you to the success you are destined for and help you win the championship. Expect a miracle and follow your dreams. They will come true. It's not just time to play. It's time to WIN!

Available on Amazon.com, Barnes N Noble, Books A Million, Legacy Bookstore, and other global retailers.

Contact Information for Charlotte Crumley Arrington

Instagram
@thekissingflightattendant
@expectamiracle108

Facebook
Charlotte Crumley Arrington
The Message 108
The Kissing Flight Attendant

Website
www.expectamiracle108

CPSIA information can be obtained
at www.ICGtesting.com
Printed in the USA
LVHW070511081221
705577LV00008B/70

9 781737 349495